ANDREA D. PRICE

Everyday Prayers for Servant Leaders

Best wishes as you continue
to grow as a servant
leader.

West Little Rock Civitan

First published by Bridge Builders Group, LLC in 2018

Maggie Carroll - Author Photograph

Library of Congress Control Number: 2018913257

All Scripture quotations are taken from the King James Version of the Bible.

Quantity discounts are available when purchased in bulk (minimum of 10) for corporate use, author events, resale/wholesale.

To order in bulk, please email prayers@andreadprice.com. Your request will be answered within 3 business days.

Monticello, Arkansas

First edition

ISBN: 978-0-578-41035-7

Cover art by Fred Nash
Editing by Shannon M. Lake

This book was professionally typeset on Reedsy.
Find out more at reedsy.com

Everyday Prayers for Servant Leaders is dedicated to my late father, John Wesley Smith. My dad faithfully served Mt. Pleasant AME Church, Bartholomew #28 Prince Hall Masonic Lodge, and Drew County Little League Baseball and Pee Wee Basketball.

John Wesley Smith
January 9, 1950 – August 22, 2018

Contents

Preface

Servant (ser·vant) **Leader** (lead·er) *A person who gives priority to the needs of those they serve.*

"Much prayer, much power. Little prayer, little power. No prayer, no power." This is a mantra I heard over and over again as a kid growing up in Arkansas. Prayer, as a necessary act of faith, was instilled in me early, and I always trusted that prayer is an essential part of Christian life and life as a servant leader.

By age 35, I was living out my dreams of being a professional servant leader. I'd worked as a teacher, founded and led a nonprofit organization, and volunteered in the United States and abroad. I even earned a master's degree in Public Service. Optimism drove my passion, and my love for humanity drove my commitment.

Unfortunately, along my service journey, I became weary and discouraged. Not because I didn't believe that there was value in my work, but because I disconnected from my service purpose. During this time, I needed to re-plug into the faith that served as the catalyst for my work. I remembered the "more prayer more power" mantra, and I began to write my prayers.

I've always prayed verbally and through meditation, but writing prayers was something I'd never done. The week that I began writing my prayers, I received three unexpected calls to serve nonprofit directors through consultancy. As a result of reconnecting to God through prayer, I started to trust God's purpose for me and to appreciate the gift of being a servant leader.

Servant leadership has taught me many things, but one lesson that I've learned is that leaders need encouragement, support, and direction. Yes, being a servant leader is rewarding, but it can also be challenging. That's why prayer is an essential part of servant leadership.

My hope is that the words from these prayers touch you in a way that strengthens you, encourages you, and motivates you to grow in your faith and service.

Yours in service,

Andrea D. Price

Acknowledgement

Dr. Elvin T. Price, Henry Price, Heidi Price, Sarah Smith. Thank you all so much for your support!

Fear

There is no fear in love, but perfect love casts out fear. For fear has to do with punishment, and whoever fears has not been perfected in love. 1 John 4:18

Dear God,

Thank you for this opportunity to allow your perfecting love to drive out the fears that stand between me and your expectations of me. Strengthen my confidence that comes from you. Help me to answer the question, "What would I do if I knew that I could not fail?" because sometimes fear of failure stands between my destiny and me. Since there is no fear in love and you are LOVE, Lord, I ask for courage. I will serve you and your people, and I pray for your strength as I do your work, without fear. Because you live, I can face tomorrow. Because you live, all fear is gone. Lord, I thank you for driving out fear.

Amen.

What would you do if you knew you could not fail?

To Do List

He who was seated on the throne said, "I am making everything new!" Then he said, "Write this down, for these words are trustworthy and true." Revelation 21:5

Dear God,

Help me to use my time wisely. Help my "to do" list align with the work you want me to do. Help me to prune away the things in my life that are dead or will produce no fruit. Lord, help my time spent in your service to be productive and give me the energy to do the work according to your will. You are a provider, God. You provide the time, the energy, and the direction for me, and I am thankful.

Amen.

What things need pruning in your life?

Planning

For which of you, intending to build a tower, sits not down first, and counts the cost, whether he have sufficient to finish it? Luke 14:28

Dear God,

You are the Master Planner. You planned the world. You planned my life. You planned the type of service that you called me to give. Lord, proper planning prevents poor service, so I ask that you direct all of my plans. Lord, I pray that everything that I plan is good and will give you all the glory and all the praise.

Amen.

How can faith direct your planning?

Coworkers

And whatsoever ye do, do it heartily, as to the Lord, and not unto men. Colossians 3:23

Dear God,

Thank you for giving me a community of co-workers. We come from different backgrounds, different experiences, and have different personalities, but despite our differences, we are here at the same place at the same time for a reason. Lord, help me to see you in each one of them. Lord, provide us with the tools, resources, and knowledge to work with each other in harmony and love. Strengthen us where we are weak, and if or when there is friction between us, give us the resolve to turn that friction into better service.

Amen.

How can your relationships with coworkers be improved?

Creativity

For we are his workmanship, created in Christ Jesus unto good works, which God hath before ordained that we should walk in them. Ephesians 2:10

Dear God,

You, the Master Creator, created me in your image. Not only did you create me, but you also made me a creative vessel for your work. Lord, I ask that creativity manifest itself through my service. When the conventional won't do, give me a fresh, unique approach to my service.

Amen.

What role does creativity play in your servant leadership?

Provision

And God is able to make all grace abound toward you; that ye, always having all sufficiency in all things, may abound to every good work. 2 Corinthians 9:8

Dear God,

Thank you for your provision. Sometimes I focus on the things I don't have rather than what you have already provided. Lord as I center my mind and heart on you, help me to remember that what I need, you provide. You provided deliverance for Daniel in the lion's den. You provided healing for the woman with the issue of blood. You provided for your disciples. You provide for me and those I serve, and I thank you!

Amen.

What has God provided for you?

I Am Enough

But by the grace of God I am what I am...1 Corinthians 15:10

Dear God,

You created me, and I am enough. Lord, thank you for equipping me with everything that makes me, me. In my failures, I am enough. In my successes, I am enough. In my disappointment, I am enough. In my jubilation, I am enough. In my service, I am enough. Lord, you created me in your image. I am enough. In those times where I feel like I am not enough, redirect my thinking, adjust my attitude, and help me to never doubt that I am enough.

Amen.

How are you enough?

Meetings

Let no corrupt communication proceed out of your mouth, but that which is good to the use of edifying, that it may minister grace unto the hearers. Ephesians 4:29

Dear God,

As I lead this meeting, I ask that each person in this room take something positive from this experience. Lord, give me the words to say, the patience to listen, and the wisdom to lead this meeting. This meeting is in your hands, and I thank you for giving me this opportunity to serve.

Amen.

How do you faithfully prepare for meetings?

Weariness

And let us not be weary in well doing: for in due season we shall reap, if we faint not. Galatians 6:9

Dear God,

Sometimes I wonder if what I am doing really matters or if it will make a difference for those I serve. In those times, I think of Fannie Lou Hamer and what her service meant. I think of Rev. Dr. Martin Luther King, Jr. and what his service meant. I think of Dorothy Height and what her service meant. These examples help me with my weariness, and I thank you for giving me examples of people who gave their all to serve others. Lord, I know that you wouldn't call me to do it if you weren't going to see me through it. I thank you, and I love you.

Amen.

How do you overcome weariness?

Courage

Be strong and of a good courage, fear not, nor be afraid of them: for the Lord thy God, he it is that doth go with thee; he will not fail thee, nor forsake thee. Deuteronomy 31:6

Dear God,

In those times where I know you have given me direction, give me the courage to move, to act. Give me the courage to serve wholeheartedly. Give me the courage to speak up when I should. Give me the courage to stay quiet when I should. Give me the courage to walk boldly into a world where my courage is necessary to do what you've called me to do.

Amen.

When has courage helped you serve better?

Joy

Then he said unto them, Go your way, eat the fat, and drink the sweet, and send portions unto them for whom nothing is prepared: for this day is holy unto our Lord: neither be ye sorry; for the joy of the Lord is your strength. Nehemiah 8:10

Dear God,

You are the center of my joy, and everything that is good and everything that is perfect comes from you. When I have small wins while serving your people, I don't take that lightly, but I rejoice. When I make mistakes in my service, I don't take that lightly, but I rejoice and ask for lessons and directions. In the ups and the downs, in the wins and loses, I rejoice. When I begin to lose my joy, please restore it in a way that only you can. Lord, your joy is my health and strength and knowing this gives me comfort.

Amen.

How has the joy in service given you strength?

Strength

I can do all things through Christ which strengthens me. Philippians 4:13

Dear God,

Thank you for being the source of my strength. I know that when I am weak, only you can make me strong. You gave Nelson Mandela strength. You gave Ida B. Wells strength. You gave Harriet Tubman strength. You give me strength. I know that all my strength comes from you. Lord, when I am weak, thank you for allowing me to lean on you.

Amen.

As a servant leader, where do you find your strength?

Endurance

I have fought a good fight, I have finished my course, I have kept the faith. 2 Timothy 4:7

Dear God,

Lord, when things get hard, help me not to quit, but to keep running this service race with endurance. Help me find endurance in that safe, secret place of yours, under the shadow of the Holy Spirit. Lord, the race isn't given to the swift nor the strong, but to those who endure. Thank you for making me an endurer.

Amen.

What does endurance mean to you?

Culture

But a certain Samaritan, as he journeyed, came where he was: and when he saw him, he had compassion on him. Luke 10:33

Dear God,

The works that I do, strategies that I attempt to implement, and the service that I give are dependent on the culture of the people who I serve. I ask that as I serve, I meet every culture with the love, understanding, and compassion that only you can give me.

Amen.

What role does culture play in your leadership experience?

Thanksgiving

Rejoice evermore. Pray without ceasing. In every thing give thanks: for this is the will of God in Christ Jesus concerning you. 1 Thessalonians 5:16-18.

Dear God,

Thank you! Thank you! Thank you! If I had a million tongues, I couldn't thank you enough. Thank you for your greatness. Thank you for your blessings. Thank you for your grace and mercy. Thank you for your faith in me. Thank you for your love for me. Thank you for the lessons. Thank you for the ups. Thank you for the downs. And for those things I haven't thanked you for, thank you for them too. Renew my spirit of thanksgiving daily, so I will never forget to give you the thanks.

Amen.

What are you thankful for?

Teamwork

Two are better than one; because they have a good reward for their labor. Ecclesiastes 4:9

Dear God,

You made Ruth and Naomi a strong team. You made Mary and Jesus a strong team. As I do service work, I know that I can't do it alone. I ask that the team of people that I serve with replace conflict with understanding, replace negativity with positivity, and replace fear with faith. Help us use our collective talents and gifts wisely so that we will be a strong team and serve with excellence.

Amen.

How has teamwork affected your servant leadership?

Adaptability

And be not conformed to this world: but be ye transformed by the renewing of your mind, that ye may prove what is that good, and acceptable, and perfect, will of God. Romans 12:2

Dear God,

The only constant is change, and as things out of my control change, Lord, I want to be adaptable. I don't want to be so inflexible to change that I get stuck, or afraid, or ornery. Help me always adapt in a way that is healthy, wise, and aligned with your expectations.

Amen.

As a leader, how have you adjusted to change?

Rest

I will say of the Lord, He is my refuge and my fortress: my God; in him will I trust. Psalms 91:2

Dear God,

You are the creator and sustainer of the earth. Even in your omnipotence, you still rested. Lord, sometimes, I am so engulfed in service that I forget to rest. Lord, teach me how to rest so that I can serve others with a fresh perspective, with more energy, and with great enthusiasm.

Amen.

How can you incorporate more time for rest into your schedule?

Listening

Wherefore, my beloved brethren, let every man be swift to hear, slow to speak, slow to wrath. James 1:19

Dear God,

As I listen for your voice, I ask that you help me also listen to those I serve. Lord, help me not just to listen to hear but listen to understand. Lord, help me not only to listen to words but listen to what is said. Allow my ears, mind, and heart to open, so I can discern the messages that are relayed.

Amen.

How has listening made you an effective leader?

Activists

Learn to do well; seek judgment, relieve the oppressed, judge the fatherless, plead for the widow. Isaiah 1:17

Dear God,

I ask for strength, patience, wisdom, and endurance for everyone who works to bring positive change to people and communities.

Amen.

Why is activism important?

Energy

And being in an agony he prayed more earnestly: and his sweat was as it were great drops of blood falling down to the ground.
Luke 22:44

Dear God,

Some days I am tired, and I have nothing left to give. I can't use my own energy, but you give me the energy that I need to do your work. Lord, teach me to lean and depend on you totally, so when I am tired, I find energy in you.

Amen.

How do you renew your energy?

Lead Me

For thou art my rock and my fortress; therefore for thy name's sake lead me, and guide me. Psalms 31:3

Dear God,

Lead me, guide me along the way, if you lead me, I can't stray. Lord, you are my compass, and I need your direction in my service to others. I can't serve without your guidance, and I need you every minute and every hour to direct my works. I thank you for being my compass because I am lost without you.

Amen.

As a servant leader, where do you look for leadership?

Empathy

And be ye kind one to another, tenderhearted, forgiving one another, even as God for Christ's sake hath forgiven you. Ephesians 4:32

Dear God,

You see my faults, and you still love me. You know my shortcomings, and you still love me. You know all of my secrets, and you still love me. You know my pain, and you still love me. The empathy that you show me releases tension. It puts me at ease. It makes me feel safe. Lord, I ask that you strengthen my empathy muscle so that I can show others the loving empathy that you show me. Expand my capacity for empathy so that those I serve will know that I love them, I can help ease tension, and that they are safe with me.

Amen.

What role does empathy play in your servant leadership?

Community

Behold, how good and how pleasant it is for brethren to dwell together in unity! Psalms 133:1

Dear God,

Cover the community that I serve. Protect and guide everyone who makes up this community. Lord, when the community wants to focus on problems, lead us to solutions. When the community wants to focus on what happened in the past, help us learn from past mistakes and find hope in brighter futures. Give us the wisdom to understand and live the UNITY in comm'unity'. Lord, it is good and pleasant when all of your children live peacefully and lovingly together in our communities. Help all of us embody your desires for this community.

Amen.

How can your leadership bring unity to the community you serve?

Public Servants

Therefore, my beloved brethren, be ye steadfast, unmovable, always abounding in the work of the Lord, forasmuch as ye know that your labor is not in vain in the Lord. 1 Corinthians 15:58

Dear God,

Service is an act that has the power to strengthen bonds, changes lives, and heal communities. Lord, as millions of people, every day, give their time and talents in the name of service, go with each of them. Guide their ways, strengthen their resolve, and keep their hearts and minds in your loving hands as they serve.

Amen.

How has someone's service affected your life?

Sadness

And God shall wipe away all tears from their eyes; and there shall be no more death, neither sorrow, nor crying, neither shall there be any more pain...Revelation 21:4

Dear God,

I am sad. Lord, tears roll down my cheeks as I think about the suffering I see and the hurt I feel. I am overwhelmed when people are gunned down in the streets, when children are taken from the arms of their parents, and when unjust laws prevent people from living lives with freedom. Lord, help me turn this sadness into productive service. Service can change suffering. Service will wipe the tears away. Service is how I can help spread love and joy where suffering and subjugation abound. Lord, help me not be stuck in sadness, but rather let this sadness be a start of good work.

Amen.

How can you use sadness to fuel your service?

Power

And he said unto me, My grace is sufficient for thee: for my strength is made perfect in weakness. Most gladly therefore will I rather glory in my infirmities, that the power of Christ may rest upon me. 2 Corinthians 12:9

Dear God,

You are all powerful. Thank you for sharing just a small fraction of your power with me. Lord, strengthen my power to be humble. Strengthen my power to love. Strengthen my power to forgive. Strengthen my power to worship. Strengthen my power to give. Strengthen my power to have empathy. Strengthen my power to help. Strengthen my power to serve.

Amen.

What makes you a powerful leader?

Choices

Enter ye in at the straight gate: for wide is the gate, and broad is the way, that leads to destruction, and many there be which go in thereat: Because strait is the gate, and narrow is the way, which leads unto life, and few there be that find it. Matthew 7:13-14

Dear God,

Rosa Parks chose a bus. Maya Angelou chose a pen. LeBron James chose a school. Lord, give me the wisdom to make choices, just as these leaders, that allow me to humbly serve. As I think about how you've shown that small acts of service have huge impacts on our world, I ask that you lead my choices. I put my choices in your hands, and I thank you for your direction.

Amen.

What impactful choices have you made?

Rememberance

And he took bread, and gave thanks, and brake it, and gave unto them, saying, This is my body which is given for you: this do in remembrance of me. Luke 22:19

Dear God,

I will never forget and will always embrace your love, your care, and all of the lessons you've given me in your Holy Word. Lord, as I remember your goodness, help me never forget that you have given me the charge to serve. With the allotted time that you have given me, I want to remember why I serve, so that I will always have the love, enthusiasm, and drive for serving others.

Amen.

What is your earliest memory of servant leadership?

Change

To everything there is a season, and a time to every purpose under the heaven. Ecclesiastes 3:1

Dear God,

I know a change is going to come. When it happens, I want to be ready to accept and embrace the change. I ask that you lead me and other servant leaders through the changing landscape of the communities we serve. I pray that I never become too stiff for change. I pray that whatever change efforts I am a part of will be beneficial for the building of a more just world.

Amen.

What changes are you preparing for?

Death

And whosoever lives and believes in me shall never die. Believest thou this? John 11:26

Dear God,

Many things die. Plants die. Bad habits die. Animals die. Relationships die. Jobs even die, but Lord, when those I serve die, it is hard to reconcile their death with the love and care I have for them. Lord, help me deal with death in a way that doesn't kill me.

Amen.

How do you deal with death?

Education

All scripture is given by inspiration of God, and is profitable for doctrine, for reproof, for correction, for instruction in righteousness. 2 Timothy 3:16

Dear God,

You taught us that people perish from the lack of knowledge. Direct me in the right way so that I can receive the tools, experiences, and education that will allow me to serve best.

Amen.

What tools, experiences, and education do you need to become a better servant leader?

Mold Me

But now, O Lord, thou art our father; we are the clay, and thou our potter; and we all are the work of thy hand. Isaiah 64:8

Dear God,

You are the potter, and I am the clay. I pray that I never become so hardened in my ways that you can't mold me to be the kind of servant leader you want me to be. I am available to you.

Amen.

In what areas do you need more molding?

Back to the Basics

But seek ye first the kingdom of God, and his righteousness; and all these things shall be added unto you. Matthew 6:33

Dear God,

When I feel consumed by my service, take me back to the basics. When I don't have the answers to the problems that I face, direct me back to the basics. When I know things should be simple, but I make them hard, take me back to the basics. The basics are your Word, your love, and your direction. Lord, keep me connected to these basic parts of my faith.

Amen.

When things get complicated, how do you go back to the basics?

Anxiety

Casting all your care upon him; for he cares for you. 1 Peter 5:7

Dear God,

When my heart flutters or my palms start to sweat, help me find calmness. When my thoughts overtake rationale, help me find peace. Help me find rest from anxiety in the grass of the meadow and lead me beside the quiet stream. Lord, restore my soul as I find peace.

Amen.

What makes you anxious and how do you find peace?

Alignment

How precious also are thy thoughts unto me, O God! how great is the sum of them! Psalms 139:17

Dear God,

Help my thoughts align with you. Help my service align with you. Help my actions align with you.

Amen.

What does alignment mean to your service?

Best

And whatsoever ye do, do it heartily, as to the Lord, and not unto men. Colossians 3:23

Dear God,

When I feel that I can't do everything I'm tasked to do, remind me that I should just do my best.

Amen.

What or who brings out the best in your service?

Advocate

If ye abide in me, and my words abide in you, ye shall ask what ye will, and it shall be done unto you. John 15:7

Dear God,

It is a big responsibility to advocate for others. Go with everyone who bears this responsibility. Go with each advocate as they serve as vessels for your service. Guide their actions, guide their words, guide their emotions, and guide their service.

Amen.

How has advocacy impacted your life?

Glory

Let your light so shine before men, that they may see your good works, and glorify your Father which is in heaven. Matthew 5:16

Dear God,

Glory to your name, your precious name. Decrease me and increase you. Lord in my service, you get the glory. In my giving, you get all the glory. In my deeds, you get the glory.

Amen.

How do you glorify God through your service?

Clarity

The entrance of thy words gives light; it gives understanding unto the simple. Psalms 119:130

Dear God,

When things get confusing, give me clarity. When I experience chaos, give me clarity. When I don't know what my next move is, give me clarity. When I reach a breaking point, give me clarity.

Amen.

How do you seek clarity?

Unbelief

Thou wilt keep him in perfect peace, whose mind is stayed on thee: because he trusts in thee. Isaiah 26:3

Dear God,

I kneel in deep contrition as I struggle with unbelief. Lord, as I struggle with unbelief in myself, I inadvertently doubt my belief in you. Lord, you have given me permission to give all of my concerns to you, and I pray that you help my unbelief. Give me all that I need to trust you and your word so that belief will be the driving force for my service.

Amen.

How do you strengthen your unbelief?

Disappointment

And we know that all things work together for good to them that love God, to them who are the called according to his purpose. Romans 8:28

Dear God,

When things don't go the way I want them to, don't allow my disappointment to be my destiny. Lord, you are the giver of hope in disappointment. You are my direction when I face disappointment. You are my joy in the face of disappointment. Lord, thank you for changing my disappointment to discovery. Help me discover a better way to serve, so disappointment becomes a distant memory.

Amen.

How do you deal with disappointment?

Faith

Now faith is the substance of things hoped for, the evidence of things not seen. Hebrews 11:1

Dear God,

Thank you for giving me a faith that is so strong that it can influence the faith of others. Lord, the mustard seed faith that I have is powerful enough to move mountains, to change communities, and make the world just a little bit better. I am a proud soldier of the cross, and through service, I am able to take your love higher and higher by giving others what you have given me, unconditional love. Lord, let my faith forever be a reflection of you.

Amen.

How has the faith you bring to your servant leadership helped others?

Elected Officials

When the righteous are in authority, the people rejoice: but when the wicked bears rule, the people mourn. Proverbs 29:2

Dear God,

Thousands of people are elected to serve communities and nations all over the world. Lord, go with those leaders and help them serve those that they represent with integrity, honesty, and with love. Help them realize that their duty is public service and give them the wisdom to do no harm to those that they serve.

Amen.

Think of an elected official who exemplifies servant leadership. What characteristics make them a strong leader?

Productivity

In all labor there is profit: but the talk of the lips tend only to penury. Proverbs 14:23

Dear God,

Is my service in vain? No. Lord, help my service be productive. I don't want to be like a hamster in a wheel, but I want my work to lead to something greater for those I've been called to serve. Give me the insight to see the habits that I need to break and the changes I need to make so that I am productive. Thank you for being a prayer answerer.

Amen.

What steps can you take to make sure your servant leadership is productive?

Abundance

Thou preparest a table before me in the presence of mine enemies: thou anointed my head with oil; my cup runs over. Psalms 23:5

Dear God,

Thank you for giving me abundant life. Lord, when I feel like I am operating at a deficit, help me to remember that my life is abundant. This abundance is not just for me, but it is for me to share in the way I walk, talk, shine, lead and live.

Amen.

What does living in abundance mean to you?

Righteousness

Little children, let no man deceive you: he that doeth righteousness is righteous, even as he is righteous. 1 John 3:7

Dear God,

I am afraid of not being in your will. When I do things my way, I don't trust that my decisions will always be your will. Lord, as I try my hardest to stay in your will, protect me from my selfish desires so that my service is led by you.

Amen.

How do you live a righteous life?

Comfort Zone

For the prophecy came not in old time by the will of man: but holy men of God spake as they were moved by the Holy Ghost. 2 Peter 1:21

Dear God,

Help me to take risks and leave my comfort zone. Lord, in my comfort zone, I get complacent and stagnant, two things I don't want. Lord, expand my thoughts so that my mind is renewed and my experiences expanded.

Amen.

What happens when you stay in your comfort zone?

Persistence

Therefore, my beloved brethren, be ye steadfast, unmovable, always abounding in the work of the Lord, forasmuch as ye know that your labor is not in vain in the Lord. 1 Corinthians 15:58

Dear God,

Help me to persistently do my best.

Amen.

How are you persistently your best?

Challenges

My brethren, count it all joy when ye fall into divers temptations; Knowing this, that the trying of your faith works patience. James 1:2-3

Dear God,

I know that challenges will come, but I also know that you want me to still go to you. Lord, help me face whatever challenges come my way with finesse and grace.

Amen.

How do you face challenges?

Availability

And Jesus said unto them, Come ye after me, and I will make you to become fishers of men. And straightway they forsook their nets, and followed him. Mark 1:17-18

Dear God,

I am available to you. My will, I give to you. I am an empty vessel, and I trust you to fill me up every day. You fill me with love for others. You fill me with a spirit of service. You fill me with purpose. Thank you! Thank you! Thank you!

Amen.

How do you make yourself available?

Disinherited

The Lord also will be a refuge for the oppressed, a refuge in times of trouble. Psalms 9:9

Dear God,

You are God of the disinherited. You are God of the oppressed. You are God to everyone that society has turned its back on. Lord, give the disinherited power, strength, courage, support and your love. Go with everyone who cares for the disinherited. Lord, bless their work, their leadership, and their commitment.

Amen.

How do you care for the disinherited?

Omnipotent

The eyes of the Lord are in every place, beholding the evil and the good. Proverbs 15:3

Dear God,

You are everywhere, at all times. Thank you for being omnipotent. I don't have to do much searching to find you, because you are always here. Lord, help me see you in this lost world. Having you as an ever-present help in a troubled world is comforting.

Amen.

How is God's omnipotence comforting for you?

Heartbreak

The Spirit of the Lord God is upon me; because the Lord hath anointed me to preach good tidings unto the meek; he hath sent me to bind up the brokenhearted, to proclaim liberty to the captives, and the opening of the prison for them that are bound. Isaiah 61:1

Dear God,

Time after time, the broken and broken-hearted try to break others. Even those who serve face heartbreak. When hearts heal, people begin to experience the fullness of human love. Lord, you are a healer, and I ask that you heal the hearts of the broken-hearted.

Amen.

How do you deal with heartbreak?

Action

But whoso looks into the perfect law of liberty, and continues therein, he being not a forgetful hearer, but a doer of the work, this man shall be blessed in his deed. James 1:25

Dear God,

Help me continue...
- A-Acting in accordance with your direction
- C-Connecting with others who serve
- T-Trusting my gifts
- I-Ignoring idleness
- O-Optimistically serving others
- N-Never leaving your side as I serve.

Amen.

What actions do you take to serve others?

Temptation

Watch and pray, that ye enter not into temptation: the spirit indeed is willing, but the flesh is weak. Matthew 26:41

Dear God,

As I serve others, protect me from temptations that distract me from my service call. Give me the strength and power that I need to keep me from yielding to temptation.

Amen.

What temptations keep you from serving?

Discernment

And this I pray, that your love may abound yet more and more in knowledge and in all judgment; That ye may approve things that are excellent; that ye may be sincere and without offence till the day of Christ. Philippians 1:9-10

Dear God,

Help me to know what things I need to know. Help me to see what I need to see. Help me to understand what I need to understand. Help me to feel what I need to feel. Help me to serve where I need to serve. Help me to serve how I need to serve. Lord, I pray for discernment as I do your will.

Amen.

What role does discernment play in your service?

Transformation

Therefore if any man be in Christ, he is a new creature: old things are passed away; behold, all things are become new. 2 Corinthians 5:17

Dear God,

Transform me by renewing my mind. Lord, I need this renewal daily.

Amen.

What role does your faith play in renewing your mind?

Right Spirit

Create in me a clean heart, O God; and renew a right spirit within me. Psalms 51:10

Dear God,

Give me a right spirit so that before I speak, God, you speak for me. Before I smile, you smile for me. Before I serve, God, you serve for me. May your spirit radiate from me in such a way that there is no denying the presence of you in my service.

Amen.

What does it mean to have a clean heart?

Appreciation

We give thanks to God always for you all, making mention of you in our prayers. 1 Thessalonians 1:2

Dear God,

Help me find appreciation in things that I've ignored. The breeze. The sound of birds and insects. The smell of fresh air. The beauty of the sky. I know that if I give these things attention, and appreciate them, I will begin to enjoy other things that matter.

Amen.

How can you take time to appreciate things that you ignore, but matter?

Dreams

For I reckon that the sufferings of this present time are not worthy to be compared with the glory which shall be revealed in us. Romans 8:8

Dear God,

Give me the strength to be bold enough to dream. Lord, the future begins with a dream. My servant leadership starts with a dream. The types of service I give begin with a dream. I give because I dream. Inspire my dreams, Lord. Allow my dreams never to be deferred, but realized in a way that shows that their manifestation is a manifestation of you.

Amen.

How do your dreams inspire your service?

Vision

And the Lord answered me, and said, Write the vision, and make it plain upon tables, that he may run that reads it. For the vision is yet for an appointed time, but at the end it shall speak, and not lie: though it tarry, wait for it; because it will surely come, it will not tarry. Habakkuk 2: 2-3

Dear God,

Open all of my senses so that I can adequately serve. Lord, you provide the vision and the power for me to serve. Help me to know your vision for my service. Help me to trust the vision. Help me to implement the vision.

Amen.

What vision has God given you?

Building

Wherefore comfort yourselves together, and edify one another, even as also ye do. 1 Thessalonians 5:7

Dear God,

You are the Master Engineer. Lend me your tools so that I can build bridges through service. Lord, service connects people. Service heals wounds. Lord, as I build bridges of service, help me to do no harm. Give me the love to build. Give me the love to serve.

Amen.

How do you build bridges through service?

Humility

For whosoever exalts himself shall be abased; and he that humbles himself shall be exalted. Luke 14:11

Dear God,

I ask for humility as I grow in the gifts and talents you've given me. I know that everything I am is because of you. I humbly serve because who I am and what I do is because of you.

Amen.

What role does humility play in your service?

Organization

Let all things be done decently and in order. 1 Corinthians 14:40

Dear God,

Go with me and keep me organized. Chaos leads to confusion, and I don't want confusion. Help me keep my files organized, my meetings scheduled in a way that I'm not overworked, and my service work balanced so that I can lead effectively.

Amen.

How can you improve your organization?

Network

Iron sharpens iron; so a man sharpens the countenance of his friend. Proverbs 27:17

Dear God,

Thank you for showing me that my network is my net-worth. Opportunity after opportunity to serve has been because you gave me the chance to meet and interact with people who are also leading and serving. Lord, I ask that you continue to expand my network so that I can continue to do the work you've called me to do and serve more people.

Amen.

How has your network influenced your service?

Lifting Others

Let nothing be done through strife or vainglory; but in lowliness of mind let each esteem other better than themselves. Look not every man on his own things, but every man also on the things of others. Philippians 2:3-4

Dear God,

Every interaction that I have is an opportunity for me to lift people up and not tear them down. Lord, let my words and actions be seasoned with love, and may the flavor of my interactions be sweet.

Amen.

How do you lift others through your servant leadership?

Restoration

He restores my soul: he leads me in the paths of righteousness for his name's sake. Psalms 23:3

Dear God,

Sometimes I feel depleted, even when I know I am doing your will. Lord, you are the restorer of my soul, and I am in need of restoration.

Amen.

What makes you feel depleted and how are you restored?

Evangelism

And I, if I be lifted up from the earth, will draw all men unto me.
John 12:32

Dear God,

Show me how to evangelize through my work. Lord, when opportunities come that allow me to share the fullness of your love, help me to evangelize in a way that glorifies and lifts up your name.

Amen.

What is the connection between your work and your evangelism?

Trust

Trust in the Lord with all thine heart; and lean not unto thine own understanding. In all thy ways acknowledge him, and he shall direct thy paths. Proverbs 3:5-6

Dear God,

I put all of my trust in you. Lord, I trust that the gifts you have given me are because you know I will be a good steward of those gifts. I trust that the work you have called me to do is because you have created me for this work. I trust that you will continue to direct my steps as I do your will.

Amen.

In what ways do you trust God?

Self-Care

And in the morning, rising up a great while before day, he went out, and departed into a solitary place, and there prayed. Mark 1:35

Dear God,

I am learning more and more about the importance of self-care. I try to serve others fully, but I often forget to take care of myself. In those times of distress and those times of eustress, help me to remember to care for myself.

Amen.

How can you better incorporate self-care into your lifestyle?

Sent vs. Went

Also I heard the voice of the Lord, saying, Whom shall I send, and who will go for us? Then said I, Here am I; send me. Isaiah 6:8

Dear God,

"Some were sent, and some just went" is a phrase I heard time and time again as a child. I want to be sure that what I am doing is what you have sent me to do. I ask that you continue to direct me and guide me along the path that you prepared for me. Lord, if I try to step on a path that you have created for someone else, please guide me back on the right track.

Amen.

How do you seek clarity on your role as a servant leader?

Thoughts

Finally, brethren, whatsoever things are true, whatsoever things are honest, whatsoever things are just, whatsoever things are pure, whatsoever things are lovely, whatsoever things are of good report; if there be any virtue, and if there be any praise, think on these things. Philippians 4:8

Dear God,

I humbly ask that you align my thoughts on things that matter. Those things that find hope in hopeless situations, those thoughts that bring determination in despair, and those thoughts that bring comfort in the midst of loneliness. I ask, and I receive.

Amen.

How do you center your thoughts on things that matter?

Freedom

Stand fast therefore in the liberty wherewith Christ hath made us free, and be not entangled again with the yoke of bondage. Galatians 5:1

Dear God,

Who the Son sets free is free indeed! I pray for freedom, Lord. Free me from the stronghold of financial stress. Free me from the limits that I set for myself. Free me from anything that keeps me from doing your service.

Amen.

What do you need to be free from?

Possibilities

Is any thing too hard for the Lord? At the time appointed I will return unto thee, according to the time of life, and Sarah shall have a son. Genesis 18:14

Dear God,

Thank you for showing me what's possible by living a life dedicated to service. I've seen what's possible when people devote time and talents to causes greater than themselves. I've seen what's possible when people come together in the name of service. I've seen what's possible when love precedes service. I rejoice in the hope of what's possible.

Amen.

What's possible because of your servant leadership?

Grace

For by grace are ye saved through faith; and that not of your-selves: it is the gift of God. Ephesians 2:8

Dear God,

I willfully and thankfully accept your grace. Time after time, I've made mistakes, but because of grace, those mistakes don't define me but instead make me better. I rejoice because your grace is bigger than my mistakes!

Amen.

Why is grace important to you?

Wisdom

The heart of the prudent gets knowledge; and the ear of the wise seeks knowledge. Proverbs 18:15

Dear God,

I want wisdom. Lord, I ask that you impart wisdom in me so that my decisions will be sound, my service will be formidable, and my relationships will be fruitful.

Amen.

What knowledge do you desire?

Purpose

The thief cometh not, but for to steal, and to kill, and to destroy: I am come that they might have life, and that they might have it more abundantly. John 10:10

Dear God,

Thank you for the time that you have given me to serve. Lord, my time here is temporary, so I ask that you impart in me the wisdom that I need to serve with purpose.

Amen.

What is the purpose of your servant leadership?

Communication

Set a watch, O Lord, before my mouth; keep the door of my lips. Psalms 141:3

Dear God,

You bestowed the first disciples with such effective communication skills that they were able to spread your word in a way that has lasted for generations. I ask that you empower me to be an effective and efficient communicator. Lord, I pray that my words, my body language, my gestures, and energy help me to communicate clearly. Lord, I know that my communication should reflect you. I falter and sometimes stumble when I communicate, but I will continue to seek your face and your guidance as I continue to grow as a communicator.

Amen.

What can you do to become a better communicator?

Justice

But let judgment run down as waters, and righteousness as a mighty stream. Amos 5:24

Dear God,

May justice flow through this world like a mighty river. May its currents lift up the wrongfully accused and incarcerated, the depressed and downtrodden, the abused and disinherited. May it rage to awaken those who ignore the tragedy of injustice. May it move us towards a fairer society.

Amen.

What role does justice play in your servant leadership?

Gladness

This is the day which the Lord hath made; we will rejoice and be glad in it. Psalms 118:24

Dear God,

Thank you for surrounding me with people who show their love through service. They give me strength, encouragement, and motivation to serve with gladness.

Amen.

What makes you glad?

Focus

Let thine eyes look right on, and let thine eyelids look straight before thee. Proverbs 4:25

Dear God,

You keep me in perfect peace when I keep my mind focused on you. When I focus on you, I lead with love and make wise decisions. I pray that I am not distracted by negativity, wavering faith, or insecurities. I pray that my focus on you makes me a great leader.

Amen.

What happens when you lose focus?

Mercy

Blessed are the merciful: for they shall obtain mercy. Matthew 5:7

Dear God,

Thank you for not allowing me to reap everything I've sown. Because you are merciful, I am thankful that you give me opportunities over and over again to make mistakes, learn from them, and still find love in you. I thank you for your mercy! When I fall short in fulfilling your expectations of me, I ask that you continue to show mercy and give me guidance so that I can fulfill your calling on my life.

Amen.

How has God shown mercy to you?

Family

The wicked are overthrown, and are not: but the house of the righteous shall stand. Proverbs 12:7

Dear God,

I come to you as humbly as I know how asking that you go with my family. I'm praying for unity, protection, provision, and a whole lot of love. Lord, love is the currency that trumps everything that we will face. Give us the mental and spiritual fortitude to not be too caught up in our work, but to find time to appreciate each other and the bonds that make us family. When family bonds are weakened, I ask that you be the superglue that strengthens our relationships with each other. Lord, I pray that as I give selfless service, I still am able to give love to my family.

Amen.

How do you balance your family life and your service life?

Protection

The God of my rock; in him will I trust: he is my shield, and the horn of my salvation, my high tower, and my refuge, my savior; thou savest me from violence. I will call on the Lord, who is worthy to be praised: so shall I be saved from mine enemies. 2 Samuel 22:3-4

Dear God,

You are the Ultimate Protector. Keep me and those that I serve safe. Lord, in our travels, protect us. In our interactions, protect us. In our work, protect us. As I continue to serve, I lean into your arms of protection, and I thank you for the comfort and safety.

Amen.

What is your prayer for protection?

Forgiveness

And when ye stand praying, forgive, if ye have ought against any: that your Father also which is in heaven may forgive you your trespasses. Mark 25:11

Dear God,

Teach me how to forgive. I know the weight of unforgiveness, and it is too much to bear. I don't want to be weighed down.

Amen.

Why is forgiveness important to your servant leadership?

Beauty

And God saw everything that he had made, and, behold, it was very good. Genesis 1:31

Dear God,

Help me see the beauty in everything. Lord, everything you conceived and created is beautiful, but sometimes I am blinded and can't see the beauty. Help me see beauty in desperate situations. Help me see the beauty in blighted communities. Help me see the beauty in every person I am charged to lead.

Amen.

What is something beautiful that you never noticed?

Optimism

Blessed is the man that trust in the Lord, and whose hope the Lord is. Jeremiah 17:7

Dear God,

This is the day that you have made, and I will rejoice and be glad. Lord, I want to approach every day and every experience with optimism. When pessimism attempts to creep in, I need your power to help me crush it with the strength that only you give.

Amen.

What are you optimistic about?

Words

Let no corrupt communication proceed out of your mouth, but that which is good to the use of edifying, that it may minister grace unto the hearers. Ephesians 4:29

Dear God,

May the words of my mouth be acceptable in your sight. As I bring your love and power into my service, may my words reflect you. Before I open my mouth, give me the words to say so that each verbal interaction that I have will be a reflection of you.

Amen.

How have someone's words changed your life?

Integrity

But let your communication be, yea, yea; nay, nay. Matthew 5:37

Dear God,

I want my relationship with you to be the driving force of the decisions that I make and the actions that I take. Lord, you are the way, the truth, and the life and I ask that you fortify me so that I live my life and do my service with integrity.

Amen.

Why is integrity critical for your servant leadership?

Resourcefulness

And he commanded the multitude to sit down on the grass, and took the five loaves, and the two fishes, and looking up to heaven, he blessed, and brake, and gave the loaves to his disciples, and the disciples to the multitude. And they did all eat, and were filled: and they took up of the fragments that remain twelve baskets full. Matthew 14:19-20

Dear God,

You fed the multitude with two fish and five loaves. Lord, as I serve, help me to be resourceful so that whatever you provide, I maximize the provision. Lord, when you give me a little, show me how to be resourceful. When you provide me with a lot, show me how to be resourceful and not wasteful.

Amen.

How do you use available resources to maximize your service?

Confidence

For the Lord shall be thy confidence, and shall keep thy foot from being taken. Proverbs 3:26

Dear God,

A lack of confidence is what keeps so many of us from taking the first step to fulfill the service calling that you have placed in our lives. Lord, all of your children are safe with you, and if we truly trust you, we will always have the confidence needed to do the work you have entrusted us to do. Lord, strengthen the confidence of those who doubt themselves and in turn doubt you.

Amen.

In what area in your servant leadership do you need more confidence?

Hope

Now the God of hope fill you with all joy and peace in believing, that ye may abound in hope, through the power of the Holy Ghost. Romans 15:13

Dear God,

You are the resuscitator of hope. Lord, in this world, so many of your children are hopeless or clinging to a tiny bit of hope. I ask that you breathe the breath of life into the hopeless. I pray that you give the hopeless chest compressions of love. I pray that you shock the hopeless with the power of the Holy Spirit. I ask that you give them a new life that is rooted in hope. With hope, there is a belief in a better future. With hope, there is the freedom to dream. With hope, there is the confidence to know that life matters. Through your power, I know that you keep hope alive.

Amen.

What do you hope for?

Fun

There is nothing better for a man, than that he should eat and drink, and that he should make his soul enjoy good in his labor. This also I saw, that it was from the hand of God. Ecclesiastes 2:24

Dear God,

Teach me to incorporate more fun into my life. Lord, restore in me the freedom that I felt as a child to run, play, climb trees, and look for adventure in the simplest things such as a cardboard box. Let me not get so caught up in work, paying bills, and adulting, that I don't take time to laugh and just have fun.

Amen.

What do you do for fun?

Decisions

Seek the Lord and his strength, seek his face continually. 1 Chronicles 16:11

Dear God,

I receive power when I partner with you on the decisions that I make. Guide my decision making so that I will do no harm in my service.

Amen.

How do you make sure that your decisions, as a servant leader, do no harm to those you serve?

Compassion

And Jesus, when he came out, saw much people, and was moved with compassion toward them, because they were as sheep not having a shepherd: and he began to teach them many things. Mark 6:34

Dear God,

Without compassion, I can't be an effective servant leader. Please keep my heart and mind open so that I can faithfully serve with compassion.

Amen.

How do you show compassion through your servant leadership?

Problem-Solving

Ask, and it shall be given you; seek, and ye shall find; knock, and it shall be opened unto you. Matthew 7:7

Dear God,

There would be no need for leadership if all of the problems in this world were solved. I humbly ask that you strengthen my problem-solving skills because the service that I give impacts communities and people's lives. You are an ever-present help in times of need, and I need your help and guidance.

Amen.

Why is problem-solving essential for your leadership?

Saying Yes

For the gifts and calling of God are without repentance. Romans 11:29

Dear God,

I say "yes", Lord, "yes" to your will and to your way. I know I've questioned your assignment on my life. At times, I refused to accept some of your requests because I didn't understand my own strengths. The more I grow, the more I understand your intent for me. Lord, as I continue to grow in our relationship, I will continue to seek your guidance when I say, "Yes!"

Amen.

What do you need to "say" yes to?

Saying No

There hath no temptation taken you but such as is common to man: but God is faithful, who will not suffer you to be tempted above that ye are able...1 Corinthians 10:13

Dear God,

I am slowly beginning to understand the power of the word "no." I have overcommitted myself to things over and over again in my attempt to "save the world," but saving the world is not what I am capable of, only you have the power to do that. I ask for continued strength to say "no" when I need to say "no." I ask for continued strength to say "no" when the request is not aligned with my personal service mission. I asked for continued strength to say "no" when a "yes" will take my focus off priorities in my life.

Amen.

Have you said "no", and it kept you from overcommitting? How did saying "no" make your servant leadership stronger?

Patience

Rejoicing in hope; patient in tribulation; continuing instant in prayer. Romans 12:12

Dear God,

In my hasty ways, I ask that you give me the patience of Job.

Amen.

Who is a leader that shows great patience? How do they show patience?

Motivation

Every man according as he purposeth in his heart, so let him give; not grudgingly, or of necessity: for God loved a cheerful giver. 2 Corinthians 9:7

Dear God,

Motivate me to serve so that I can be both a good and faithful servant leader. Help me to passionately persevere and get up every day motivated to fulfill my service mission.

Amen.

What keeps you motivated to serve?

Prayer

Therefore I say unto you, What things ye desire, when ye pray, believe that ye receive them, and ye shall have them. Mark 11:24

Dear God,

You've heard this prayer throughout the generations, and it is my prayer too: "Teach me how to pray and what to pray for." Lord, in all of my petitioning to you, I know that there are some things I miss. Lord, continue to cover me even when I don't have a specific petition. You are all seeing and all-knowing, and you know what my requests are before I even make them. I thank you for being a listening ear, a vigilant eye, and a warm touch. In addition to teaching me how to pray and what to pray for, I ask that you teach those who desire to build their relationship with you how to communicate with you also.

Amen.

What is your prayer?

About the Author

ANDREA D. PRICE'S servant leadership enables her to help other servant leaders and nonprofit organizations reach their goals. She's a native of Monticello, AR, and currently resides in Virginia with her husband, Dr. Elvin Price, and two children, Henry and Heidi. She earned a master's degree in Public Service from the University of Arkansas-Clinton School of Public Service. She is a member of Delta Sigma Theta Sorority, Inc.

You can connect with me on:

🌐 https://andreadprice.com